You Know the Ones

You Know the Ones

Dave Malone

Golden Antelope Press
715 E. McPherson
Kirksville, Missouri 63501
2017

ISBN 978-1-936135-26-4 (1-936135-26-4)

Library of Congress Control Number: 2016963620

Published by:
Golden Antelope Press
715 E. McPherson
Kirksville, Missouri 63501

Available at:
Golden Antelope Press
715 E. McPherson
Kirksville, Missouri, 63501
Phone: (660) 665-0273
http://www.goldenantelope.com
Email: ndelmoni@gmail.com

Acknowledgments:

Some of these poems, often in earlier versions, were first published elsewhere. Grateful acknowledgement to the editors of these journals.

- "Course" originally appeared at the Tweetspeak poetry website (*tspoetry.com*) as part of a poetry prompt.
- *Cave Region Review*: "Middle Age" as "Glance"
- *Elder Mountain*: "Elegy for an Artist" and "Old Photograph, Town Square"
- *Flutter*: "Regret"
- *Flying Island*: "Beginnings"
- *Foliate Oak*: "Sincerest Little Love Poem" as "If"
- *Futures Trading*: "O Running Girls"
- *The Heartland Review*: "Moonshinin'"
- *Mid Rivers Review*: "Awake," "Rift," "What Is Gained," and "What Is Lost"
- *Plainsongs*: "Progress"
- *Prairie Winds*: "Tough Love"
- *Right Hand Pointing*: "Country Boy Buys Box Wine"

All photos are those of the author's with the following exceptions and are reprinted here with permission:

- *Author in West Texas, circa 1988*, Wendy Hornbaker Dooldeniya (page 13)
- *House, West Plains, Missouri, 2013*, Jennifer Wichern (page 17)
- *West Plains, Missouri, Depot, October 18, 1914*, property of Russ Cochran and the *West Plains Gazette*. Reprinted from *West Plains Gazette*, Spring/Summer, 1978, p. 58. (page 23)
- *Aid's Antique Mall and Cafe, West Plains, Missouri, 2016*, Jennifer Wichern (page 31)
- *Buffalo River, May 2011*, Jennifer Wichern (page 43)
- *Norfork Lake, June 2016*, Jennifer Wichern (page 49)
- *Us, West Plains, Missouri, May 2013*, Jennifer Wichern (page 53)

Contents

School Days and Light

It was late, late in the evening,
The lovers they were gone;
The clocks had ceased their chiming,
And the deep river ran on.
—W. H. Auden

Blind Swordsman

Mr. Okamoto believed us musicians
as much as kids. With swift stroke of *katana*,
he drew the baton into blue sharpness.
If we were unruly children, he rapped
the long sword upon his music stand,
a deep black he must have loved.
In the sweltering gymnasium,
he baited us with Beethoven—
snagging even the smallest fish.

Decked

The painful past
Of middle school
Blooms in many
Colors. Worst the
Pink of Pitts's
Lips, the loathsome
Tween adult with
Armpit hair. He
Scared us all, from
First to eighth—

Until the kid
From St. Louis
Decked him in the hall
On Christmas Eve,
The final day
Of winter makeup.

Country Boy Buys Box Wine

From a past life, I remember Danny Pitts.
His seventh-grade biceps
eclipsed the mooning eyes of boys
and sent shrill coyote barks
down the line of gym girls.
Even the coaches gasped
at his locker-room bravado—
the shocking groin outgrowth,
spools of hair thick as robin nests.

Pariah in Pink

for Gary G., wherever you may have blossomed

Spring air gushed never more perfect
for pre-teens on the academy transport.
Hushed, decadent lawns and French snacks
awaited most—but not for Gary nor me.
The sophomore should not have been a passenger
amid youth more pimpled and perplexed.
And when the prickly springs
of crunching vinyl seats
rose as sharp as teenage epithets,
the pariah in pink polo shirt,
smelling of jasmine,
bore hard into a forgotten novel.

FB Message (Imagine Please)

O we were young.
Your red hair
I didn't understand
How it could glow
When Dr. Philo Clark rambled on
About toil and trouble,
Fire burn and caldron bubble.

You never answered
My cryptic notes—
Poems perhaps—
I passed across
The aisle. But then
Your farmer father
Had already married
You to a welder.

Imagine please
How lost I was
The summer after
When you kissed me
Inside the tire swing—
Only to disappear
Moments later
Inside the manish form
Of morning fog.

Sweetness

My church-filled family
got it exactly backwards.

The skinny thighs of a girl
so young were not the sandy lot

of Sarah and her righteous hubby.
Few fruits burst sweet in this life.

At best, a spring D'Anjou—
certainly not my sins nailed

to a rotten piece of wood.
But that first girl, always present

at evening service, the innocent
maiden hands, an April pear.

Liza, Kansas City, 1988

Don't Touch

You know the ones.
Close friends, high school days.
They are best where they are.
Chiseled in time.

For me the most
It's Mike. Twig-shaped tough
Who would be, mark his words,
The Crüe's drummer.

The Kansas light
Drummed upon him
On days we shot
Hoops one on one.

But now I know
Time has beaten us
Into days of mildest
Living, slowness.

And yet on some
Sweet, brooding nights,
The gold of August:
A brisk, slam dunk.

Hitchhiker

South of Oklahoma City,
interstate grayed equal to the horizon.
while cobalt sky betrayed winter chill.
A hitchhiker in brown leather, baptized head to toe,
confronted brutal wind
where he stood
with a tiny thumb.

The middle-aged man
climbed into my teenage car
as I silenced speakers at his calves.
In seconds, he removed his gloves,
casting the fetor of vinegar into the cabin,
then confessed he was Jesus
come back to save us.

Somewhere in the Texas Panhandle,
I believed. Offered him twenty dollars—
a week of college amusement—
then the heavy clap of his door.

Regret

Western Oklahoma
blooms blue sky.
I drive to meet you
for a college dance.
Slants of sunshine help
shadow autumn farms
through distant cottonwoods.

Years later, I would regret
my nonchalance at your crimson dress
and velvet pumps. The lines
of Leonard Cohen you quoted
I mistook for false sentiment.
The copper sky of evening,
burnished into dusk.

Author in West Texas, circa 1988

Memory

for Jennifer of long ago

One afternoon in West Texas,
we drove to Buffalo Gap
and into the smoke of mesquite
and burnt mesa. On the arid bluff,
we yanked up ash and twilight
as our blanket. Then, the ague
of night and salt, in the wet blue hum
of our mouths.

At college semester's end, we crooned
the famous Crowded House tune beneath
a blood-gorged moon. On the greening quad,
we recited vows of having and holding
and penning letters over summer months
until our elbows ached. A week later,
you journeyed back to Chicago
and I to a smaller somewhere else.

Vermont Winter

Beneath lake ice,
a landlocked salmon

senses smelt and spring.
He lips a well-placed artifice

but won't be snagged by tugs
of tension or warm intentions,

and so escapes the hook
while the ice above cracks like bones

and fresh pine perfumes mud hollows
giving way to sun and forest.

Poet Spends Night in Suburban Ohio

The night spent in Worthington
was close to worthless, according

to your husband who slept upstairs
while we drained the Wild Turkey

against a snowstorm meant
for farmers tucked neatly away

in Hopper houses. He dozed
while you and I teetered

at the kitchen table, fists of snow
jabbing the windows, the shrillness

of cut glass for two night hawks
circling in the gauzy light of dawn.

House, West Plains, Missouri, 2013

O Running Girls

O running girls,
I was once like you.
Thin and lithe, without complaint.

In the half-dark,
We exchange a second's glance—

Your future painful—
Then brushed off as earth
From running spike.

Aux Arcs

The true origin of the name Ozarks, about which so much vain disputation has been indulged, has been settled once for all by an inspection of old French documents preserved in St. Louis. These speak often of hunting expeditions made my French fur-traders "aux Arcs," or "Aux Os," or "aux Kans," i.e. into the territory of the Arkansas or Osage or Kansas tribes of Indians. It was common of the early French settlers to abbreviate the Indian tribal names by using merely their first syllables.

—Robert L. Ramsay, 1952

Moonshinin'

During the Depression years,
Uncle Woody stole the spring
From god and turned water into mash
With sheriff's sugar and hog grain—
And wits, of course, when revenuers
Came callin' in city boots and slickers.

But even god believed in flame
Of oak, of Lot,
The lot Woody drew.
Because when the law played its hand,
The women played theirs—
For everyone knows
Dirty laundry cleans best
With fire and smoke
Beside an Ozark spring.

Margaret Rachel Lewis Malone and James Monroe Malone, August 6, 1936, West Fork, Arkansas

Old Photograph, Town Square

Against slurring rain
and blurred sky,
the photograph
escorts you
back in time—
to banjo, porch rocker,
and black folk
on town square.
In the background,
the railroad pushes through
like a prophet's calloused hand
and issues peace—
for a moment—
before heading west.
Black and white dwell as one,
neck and neck,
tattered suit coats
and slumping bonnets—
but no one speaks.
Though you can almost
smell Sunday breath
and hear the drizzle patter.

West Plains, Missouri, Depot, October 18, 1914
©2017 Russ Cochran

Dysmorphia Inherited

for my grandmother Lucille

I didn't want your eyes.
Sand behind the glass.

Oklahoma winters, you thumbed
Life magazines. Your father
greeted migrant families with milk,
sometimes eggs. Let them lie in throes
of hay while Hoover's nation
went to manure.

I didn't want your eyes.
Sand behind the glass.

Oklahoma City, you went to business college
where a farmer's daughter learned numbers
and a flare for fashion. And you mastered
a rotund sense of self from *Photoplay*,
models clipped and measured
against your Sunday body's best.

I didn't want your eyes.
Sand behind the glass.

Lucille Newberry Malone and James Scott Malone, 1940s

Car Wreck, November 1959

for my grandmother Lucille

You flipped the car
that autumn afternoon.
Blue skies belted
honkey-tonk arias above
old Highway 60
in southern Missouri—

yet the world was all wrong.

Perhaps you sensed
cold blood across the border
or maybe you didn't like
the diner girl's hand
on your man's denimed shoulder.

Later, you recalled how
mourning doves scrambled up
from the road. Right after—
a screeching scrimmage.
Then, wood-stove scent wafting
until you beheld the tragedy—
his neck bent like a toothpick.

Depression

Spring Ozark sky,
a yellow bruise
the tornado lifts up
beneath the skin
and tears muscle
into fraying flags.
Defeat is clearly sewn
on porch stoops,
where wood columns
become firewood
beside potholes of rain.

Dust to Dust

With voices as buttery and kind
as kindergarten teachers,
your brothers tell me
how to use the chop saw
and not leave an appendage
on the garage floor—
though I tell them
speech-to-text is here to stay.

Their Wranglers and Ropers
mark a different time—
but in the moment,
we share the labor
of hewing wood.
Steady hands
and straight cuts,
distances measured,
for your father's ramp.

Thanksgiving Deer

At your brother's house,
I relax at the kitchen island.
An innocuous pro football game
simmers on the flat screen
as unseasoned as the mashed potatoes.
His daughter, birthed of a waspy
first wife, stings her way past relatives
to find me.
"Surprise," passes through
tween lips
as she thrusts
a Walmart bag
into my lap—
freezing cold—
I peer inside
at the doe's
fuzzy nubs.
"My feet,"
she squeaks.

Progress

Early morning, the old men bunker
at the café. Thirty years ago,
they were World War II veterans,
my grandfather's claw hands among theirs.
Today, the seats fill with former Korean soldiers,
sprinkled with napalm-hearted Viet Nam men.
Their faces are wrinkled black and tan,
the fate of small-town pride.

The words slow among them
for a moment when shutter clatter
then hump slivers of sunlight
onto freshly soaped wood floors.
At a grenade's-distance
in the beauty parlor, their wives
groom progress—muted mettle
on the other side of the glass.

Aid's Antique Mall and Cafe, West Plains, Missouri, 2016

Beginnings

The two grand quilting ladies
leave their mark on the street—
one a cigarette butt,
pink with yesterday's lips,
the other a crimson handbag
catching the light just so.
Forty years back, she rode
the Panama Limited to Chicago
fresh from a divorce that never took,
her elbows back on an Ozark table
a winter later.

The smoker knows
the story as much as her own—
her husband a ghost running
through flowerbeds she weeds
at the senior center where indoors
she pokers with grace—far less lonely
than any suicide king she plays.

Course

for Gracie (1943 - 2016)

Nature is not the most difficult
though furry dog legs
yield phantom rough,
then April rain,
and finally
the knock of silence—
an interminable par five,
haunting six hundred yards
in pole-barn dark.

Dusky fairway rises and falls,
green caps on a fathomless man-made lake.
The tug of the deep fishes out the fear
you've always known—

until now. Pushing hands
through hips, your body proclaims:
if not far or fair,
then clean.

The Shepherd

My truck-drivin', omelet-eatin',
rare-steak dinin', steel-toe-boot-wearin',
Jersey-born-and-reared landlord
leans against my front porch column
with a cigarette and rubs his Angus-fed belly.
You want to be on both sides:
his and his.

I perch in a blue camping chair
as he smokes another stick of damp sawdust
and pontificates about the foul weather,
the cops who drive by when they shouldn't,
and the snake tattoo on the shoulder
of the girl who moved in next door.

He leaves me in a flurry
of fading blond hair and smoke—
yet in his front window,
a pastoral scene.
Shepherd set against
brown rolling recliner.
Thimble and needle flowing
to patch up what's never said.

The Shepherd, Part Two

My landlord's Jersey accent
rings true like something long gone.
The crisp steal of Jackie Robinson—
a fleet-footed feeling when stealing home,
a head-first slide dusted safe.
The hum of Preacher Roe's curve
slowing to the outside corner
against Joltin' Joe in October of '49,
the thwop into Campanella's new mitt—
inflexible leather ready to rattle rookies
and veterans alike.

Charming Man

for RP

On lazy Saturdays,
his kid mows the lawn

while he pots plants
in stoneware his wife bakes

as rich as shepherd's pie
I remember from back home.

He likes to smoke Dunhills
in secret and waves

whenever I look. He votes
the way he should

in this neighborhood and when
watering his hostas,

he brags he wears the same jeans
he sported in high school.

Power's Out

The radio station can go
twenty minutes. The clerk
buttressing the end of the hall,
she might go five—
her blue-shadowed eyes
betraying her single status,
a rookie bench player, intent on the
modest luxuries of home:
the microwave meal, cable TV, a drained
light beer. But the writer
in Office #28,
she can go the distance,
foraging through the dark as she lights fires
on ancient typewriter keys.

Love Language

This to the crown and blessing of my life,
The much loved husband of a happy wife ...
[Who] to the world by tenderest proof discovers
They err, who say that husbands can't be lovers.
—Anne Finch

Ancestral Ash

What was true of you at twelve
Remains the same today.
With the wind is gone your hoop skirt
Of crinoline and wire
That your mother and aunt would craft
On sleety, Ozark mornings.

What is true of you at forty
Remembers the awkward girl
Of yesterday—the firmest mouth,
Recluse's spindly legs,
Desire to skirt the color
Of myth, Confederate and pale,
Ancestral ash of none you've known.

Awake

Our peeling birch
haunts when stirred—
the stoic lover
holding on to past belief.

The western thunderstorm
rides a horse across Ozark plain.
Darkens the sun, thank god,
plunges the day into blood.

On a Sunday, you slide
fingers under bark to sail
the lonely ship to sumptuous earth.

Middle Age

High above the spring,
we traipsed among
the pocked rock
shimmed by eons of rain.
Summer wild flowers
curled up inside
blue and gray bonnets.
We made a life,
raised stone,
irrigated anemones,
delighted in occasional moss

until
you jumped—

only to surface the next day,
raging pool of eyes and hair.

Buffalo River, May 2011

Across Borders

Crossing the Tennessee border,
you wake the day into being.
A frothy mist of summer
trying to spit its way into dawn—
into experience.

The Manchester sun breaks open
like an egg and casts
an orange glow on all life.

Hundreds of miles away,
in an Ozark field, a red-wing
blackbird rides barbwire
and launches into a song
never heard.

Sincerest Little Love Poem

If I could write you a love poem,
I'd make it humble,
attach Mother Teresa's photograph,
clothe the thing in blue and white,
mumble prayers over it.

I'd fold the missive into sixteenths or so,
create an old-fashioned airplane,
and launch it from kitchen island,
pray the flight would last
past the dog bowl.

If I could write you a love poem,
I'd make it simple,
grow it from the earth,
no added sugar,
insist on natural ingredients.

I'd shovel them in your morning coffee,
spike them in your beer at night,
leave the homespun elements on fingertips,
so we could dance with them in the shower,
tuck them close when we dropped off to bed.

Just Us

As May snow hugs
the Ozark landscape,
you love the difficult
in me. The belly
of my faults that stretches
from New Madrid to bedroom.
The thirsty spring grass asks,
what begs this loving?
This cap of water that embraces
the totality of verdant blades.

Trumping the Transit, June 5, 2012

We better
the transit of Venus

when you hold me
in bed. The long rays

of your body burgeon
the afternoon light

in shadow—life unknown
on supposedly a fiery planet.

Rift

I spend all morning dwelling inside
last night's conversation in the cramped car,
the stick shift a rift between us.
You can't stand a day without me.
I can't stand suffocating
inside the heavy water of Norfork Lake—
where just a day before,
we swam like ancient fish,
knowing nothing of poison or the world.

Norfork Lake, June 2016

What Is Lost

I'll never know that girl,
The redhead with dimples—
Slender arms pushing
Her grandmother through

The coaster's waiting line.
Admission price of marriage
American-style. Lost,
I wait for the killed ride

To be resurrected.
Taut shouts of *Clear!*
By teen ambassadors
Guiding machinery of memory.

What Is Gained

Night's jowls swing wide
and let the moon slip
into the gravel ditch—
the shimmer of highly-held
rain in burning August.

Not speaking,
we hold hands
across the blue abyss
of time, planets.
Against the scent of damp earth
and the screech of barn owl,
we troll the farm—
thin flames of light
ignored in the distance.

Love Language

Passers-by, eavesdroppers,
good friends can't translate
the lovers' tongue.
Their hard-earned labor
sweated into soil
over years of civil war,
passion, and mostly victory.

The syllables may slide out
as simple as cumulus
on spring days sliding
over knob and lake.
Intonations rest on bank and pine
unheard—
except to those two bodies
who harbor the entire world.

Us, West Plains, Missouri, 2011

Love Language Revisited

Nothing changes.
For nothing is
Everything.
And you and I
Might lie and quip
We never were—

But what is known
To us is *now*,
A rural life—
In which we are
A pair of oaks
That grow the same
Amid Ozark
Spring, ready to
Wither when winter
Returns to us—
When snowy stone
Marks the myth that
One of us once
Ever lived
Separately.

Love Language III: The Pact

Few understand
That one is none—
The bunching waves
Lapping on Norfork Lake.

Perhaps children know
Watching us hold hands
In winter water—
Me first, we sing
As bold as a Greek chorus.

Elegies and Eulogies

Every one of those unfortunates during the process of existence should constantly sense and be cognizant of the inevitability of his own death as well as of the death of everyone upon whom his eyes or attention rests.

—G. I. Gurdjieff

Ushered into the Night

for Mike Timmons (1956 - 2011)
All-American bouncer at Sonka's Pub

That boy was looking for a fight.
He'd been working out, after all.

A nearby undergrad proved shy enough
to insult with his silence.

And so the rift began.

You looked on.
A sage among the soft.

And when the bully threw the first punch—
somehow, you were already there

at his neck—your elbow taut,
a toreador's *muleta.*

Acadiana to Home

for Chance Briant (1994 - 2016)

You had to be Chance.
Big-eyed baby of the bayou.
Burgeoning into blond hair
And a jaw that eclipsed
Your look-a-like, Mr. James Dean.
You wore leather better.
But not always life,
A cumbersome tuba
Drenched in valves
When your heart could only
Hold so many.

We who go on
Ask too many questions,
For you have already
Answered them in music
But more so in giving.
For as far as France,
Many have felt your finest touch,
Your strumming benevolence,
From Acadiana across the Atlantic—
We now know as your swan song.

Elegy for an Artist

for Jonathan Woods (1979 - 2016)

In the landscape of Spring there is neither better nor worse;
The flowering branches grow naturally, some long, some short.
—Zen poem

You made me give Christ
A chance—the homely Jew
Westerners have made American.
I believe he is more like you—
Doe-eyed, curious, simple.
Slices of truth present
Like blackberry cobbler.

The last day I saw you,
Ozark summer burned
Like a morning cigarette,
And you baked beside
The Baptist Church
You painted with
Eyes black and focused.

A month later,
You were gone.
A fawn in the forest
Bled out from
Encroaching sin—
Yet like the son
Your limbs made amends,
Humus back to the earth.

I Can't Help

for photographer Bob Fleming (1946 - 2010)

but want to write you
a poem. After all,
it is you who put me
in my film place—when I cobbled
together Super 8 cartridges and a grand
from savings. You tutored me
in the fine dining and etiquette
of illuminating a face, but I exposed
the twenty-something gall
to ask if I could borrow
the expensive lights you cast
on high school seniors
against barbed-wire fence
or sycamore tree along Jack's Fork.
You replied as any well-cultured
Shakespearean actor or Ozark farmer
glued inside bib overalls would have:
"My, you're a cheeky fellow."

Little Earl

She loved you most
The one who most
Needed her love—
The golden boy,
The fallible
Newborn who cock
A-doodle-doo'd
On the first morning

And on the day
When death called.
You didn't light
Upon the farm
Where her body
Lay still as a doe
Among blackberry
And ivy.

Grave

for Hollis

The ancient oak rests
A hundred years after
The farmer's wife scattered
Her seeds of hope hence.

And from the winter's
Gloom, the roots would splinter
Into hardy stems—
Your grave's greenest gems.

Eulogy

for Hollis Edra Rowlett LeBaron (1924 - 2016)

You don't sum up
A woman's life.

You hope you lived
Inside it. That she
Paid you mind
When much deserved her attention—
Hens eyed by loping foe,
Polk greens and potatoes,
Children unnerved by adulthood.

You live with what's left—
Memory carved
In native stone.

Hollis Edra Rowlett LeBaron, November 7, 1942, Trask, Missouri

CPSIA information can be obtained
at www.ICGtesting.com
Printed in the USA
FSOW04n2130060317
31593FS